The Easiest Ways To Become A Successful Blogger

With pictures Guide

Copyright

First Printing Year: 2018
ISBN: 978-1-387-42031-5
ISBN-13: 978-1986986861

ISBN-10: 1986986861

Table Of Contents

Chapter 1: -Introduction

Definition of Blog

Blog is the type of website that is use for sharing ideas, tought, promotion of businesses through contents writing online.
Blog helps writers to publish their passion online. Blog can be accessed by anybody, Blog is meant to give literary information to people's.

Who Can Blog?

Anyone can blog; blog is meant for peoples that have passion for writing. If you have passion for writing; then, you can blog. But before starting a blog the first thing that need to be considered is the **Niche**.
Niche mean Subject, Area you are good at, in terms of Knowledge.
Example of Niche; Business, Sport, Life Style, Entertainment, Job, News, Politics etc.
If you are good in business, you can start a business blog or if you are good in More Than two categories of the niche you you can combine them together. If you are good in writing News, you can start a news blog.

Browsers That You Can Use For Blogging;

There are many browsers that support blogging, but opera mini doesn't really support but you can still post on your blog with opera mini using this link
https://www.blogger.com/blog-this.g
you can use Either your Phone or Computer but some of the features does not work in some mobile phones except computer.
Note: when using a mobile phone for blogger trying using you normal browser, if you don't have any other better browser.

How Does Blogging Work;

Blogging is very important to anybody ready to achieve new thing.
There are many things you can do with blog. Below are some of the things you can do with a blog:
1. Promotion of Business
2. To Promote a Particular Information to a targeted people.

3. For Person Interest
4. For Person and Earning Money. Etc

Promotion of Business

Some peoples go into blogging just to promote their business, new product update to the peoples online. It can help the business to grow fast because it is open to the peoples worldwide.

To Promote a Particular Information to a Targeted people

Some goes into blogging for a particular reason, some want to target a particular people with a certain information. And that can be done through blogging.

For Personal Interest

some go into blogging just for their own personal interest. Anything that concern business activities, blogging can make it easier and you can get whatever you want through blogging to satisfy yourself.

For Passion

some go into blogging just because of the passion they have for writing and for a particular subject.

Earning Money

It's easy and necessary for people to earn money through blogging.
There are many ways for people to earn money from their blog. Here are the List:
- Affiliate marketing Program
- Promoting other People's business
- Designing for Others
- Information Marketing
- Pay Per Click Program etc.

Affiliate Marketing Programs

This Program allow you to promote other people's products online.
There are many affiliate marketing websites eg www.amazon.com - worldwide.
www.jumia.com www.konga.com etc -Nigeria and other african countries. You can search for more online through search engines.

How To Setup The Program

Visit any of the above website, Locate the affiliate program page or search on Google to get the direct link. Sign up for the program fill all the necessary form there, then submit the application. Some will review it for days while some will not. If you account is approved visit the website, select any of their products you like, then you will be given a code, it can be text ad or banner. Text ad only displays the ad in text and it's easy to see in any low standard browser. While banner displays both the text and image. This is best in a website. Copy the code paste it in any side of your blog you want it to appear. You can share the link on Facebook, twitter and any social media of forum. If anyone click on the link and order for any of their product through the link you will be paid a commission from it. They pays into you local bank account.

Promotion of Other People Products or Business

You can make money with your blog by promoting other people's businesses on you website. Many companies would like to pay you just to place the advert of their products on your website. if they like it and they like your services.

Designing For Others

You can make money by designing blog for other people's. It is very profitable. There are many peoples looking for someone to help them get a blog. This is one method i use to make money. I design for them and they pay me. Both online and offline.

Information Marketing

Information Marketing allow you to market your ideas, knowledge on your website. You can create a book package it with relevant information and market it on you blog. It can be in pdf, doc format etc.

Pay Per Click Programs

Pay Per Click Program is the best method one can make money blogging.
This Programs allow you to place adverts on your website, if anyone click on the ad they pay you.
This program is the fastest way to make money blogging.
There are many pay per click programs eg:
www.clicksor.com -if you register here they give you code, place the code on your website and if any one click on it they pay you.
Www.media.net -this one is the same as clicksor.com and it pays better.
Www.google.com/adsense -Google Adsense is a program own by Google. This program is the best (PPC) program. It's the hope of every blogger.
Google Adsense pays higher but the problem is that, they are difficult to get an account approved. That is why i listed the two alternative programs above: media.net and clicksor.com they are not paying like Google adsense. But don't worry at the end of this book you will know how to get adsense approval quickly.

What Is Google Adsense?

Google Adsense is a pay per click program own by Google. This program displays ads on your site and if any of your visitor click on the ad they pay you. The amount of visitors you have and the effort to create contents determine how your earning will be.

Things To Consider Before Applying For Adsense

Note: before you apply for adsense there are some things you need to consider;

1. A Website; or a Blog;

You must have a website or blog with a good design that will be easy for peoples to navigate into your site. you will learn how to design the kind of website needed by adsense in this book.

Your website must be at least 6 months old:

but it's not compulsory for your website to be at least 6 months old, but in the country like china, india, its compulsory.

2. Quality Contents:

your website must have a quality contents. originally written by you, not copied. make sure that you are the true writer of the contents in your site, you can make references from other people's contents but you must write it in your own way.

3. Have At Least 30-50 Quality Contents on your Site:

You must have enough posts on your site before you can apply for adsense.

4. Have The About us, contact us, and Privacy Policy pages on Your site:

About Us page describe your website, Contact Us; mean your contact details and privacy policy have to do with how you use the information collected from your visitors; like when they comments, send message on your site etc.

5. Finally: A Custom Domain Name:

A custom Domain Name give readers the direct access to your site. eg .com .org .ga .ng .tv .com.ng etc. for example when you register for a website, they will give you a subdomain name, eg when you register with blogger; www.yoursiite.blogspot.com the .blogspot.com is the sub-domain name. if you decided to change it to a custom domain name it will be www.yoursite.com or .org etc. the .blogspot.com will be replaced with the custom domain name.
You can purchase a custom domain names from the following websites:
www.goddadys.com
www.domain.google.com
www.registeram.com etc. you can use search engine to get more,. but i will show you how to get a free domain name in this book.

if you follow the above steps, you are good to go! adsense will surely approve your application.
Note: if Adsense Disapprove your Account; check the area that you are wrong and re-apply.

Chapter 2 - How To Create A Blog

When Creating a website the first thing that should be considered is the hosting package. there are many Hosting Companies that can host your website eg www.joomla.com www.wordpress.com www.wix.com wwww.blogger.com etc.

So, We are going to use blogger to create our website.

Step 1. Visit www.gmail.com to create a gmail account if you have not, but you can use your old gmail account.

Step 2. visit www.blogger.com or www.blogsspot.com they are the same.

- **Login the Account with your gmail account.**

- **Create a profile;**

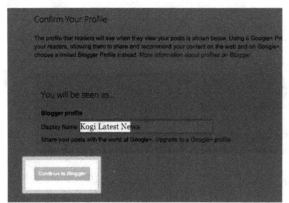

This profile contain the information about the author. any information you input will show in your site as the information about the Author.

- **Choose a profile:** if you choose google+ profile your google + profile will be linked to the site. your name on google+ will be your author Name.

if you choose create a **Limited profile:** this method you just enter the name you want it to appear as the author name. Check the picture above. Example of a limited profile.

Step 3. **Create New blog:**

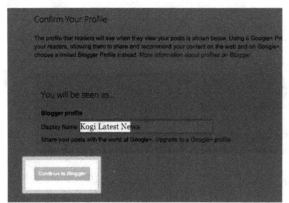

- **Click on Create New blog to to start your blog;** The Blog dialogue will open.
- **Enter the Title of your Blog;**

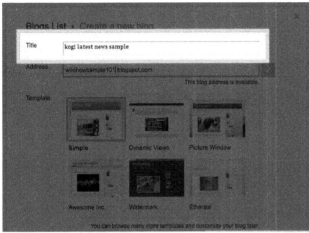

eg kogi latest news

- **Enter the url/ the address;** this blog address is the road to your site, it's through the address that people can be able to access your site. eg kogilatestnnewws.*blogspot.com* **.blogspot.com** will automatically add itself because you are yet to purchase a custom domain name.
- **Enter The Description of Your Site:** Enter a Short description about your site, eg we bring to you the latest news across the glog.
- **Select a Template:** There are many free templates on blogger, you can choose anyone to create your site but you can still change it later.

Step 4. **Now Click On Create Blog:**

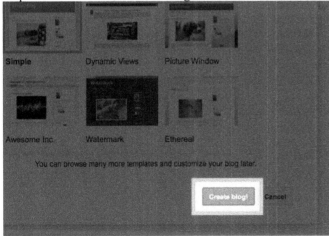

A message will come that your blog is successfully created.

you can preview to see how it look but it will not look beautiful because you haven't added anything.

How To Create A Blog Post

To create post on your blog, make sure your blogger account is logged in with the same email address you use to create the site.
Click on posts on your Blogger dashboard

- Click New post; the dialogue will open

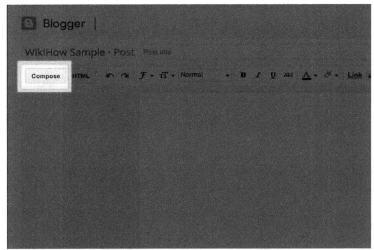

Enter Your Post Title in the small dialogue above and the body of your post in the big box

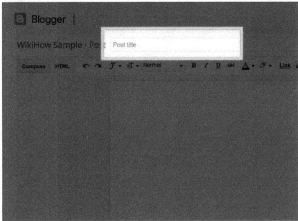

How to Create Label;

Label allow visitors to easily navigate into your site.
Click on Label

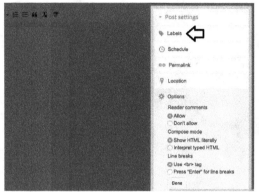

to Categorize your posts eg music, news, sport, entertainment etc.

To Add Image to Your Post

- Click on The Image Icon to upload or drag the image from your computer to the big box
- Click Publish to Publish your new post on your blog or click save to save to draft if you don't feel like to publish now or you wish to edit something later.

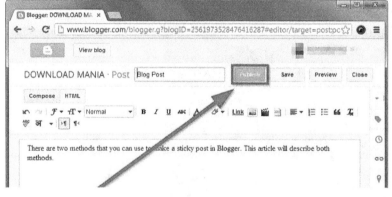

Follow the same steps to add more posts.

How To Add Audio File To Your Site

Step1: Creating Google Site for Hosting Audio File

First of all, you need to upload your audio file on external hosts as you it does not allow you to upload audio or video files. Therefore, you need to use external host to upload and I am using the most credible source and that is Google Site.

- First of all, go to Google Sites visit www.sites.google.com and Sign in using your Gmail ID and password.
- Now, click on **Create** button from top-left corner.

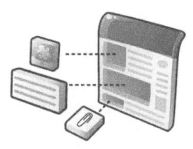

- After that, you need to give title to your site and select a template for it. You may select any template and give any name as we are only using it to host the audio file that's all. Ones you have given the name, it will auto generate the URL of your Google site; you may also change it by clicking on it and make it different from title. Now scroll down and checkmark the box, **I'm not a Robot**.
- Now, once you are done with setting up these things select **Create button** from top.

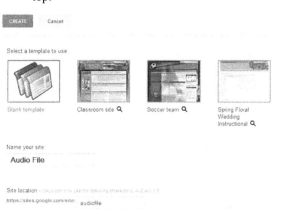

- Now your site will be created. However, you cannot add any audio or other file directly to the site. Therefore, you need to create a File Cabinet on your site to start uploading files on it.

- Now to create a file cabinet, on the same page of your site, you need to click on **Create New Page** button from top.

- Now, give title to that new page. Then you from "select a template to use" select **File Cabinet**, and lastly select **Create** button from top.

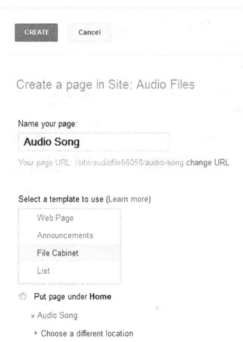

Step2: Uploading Audio File on Google Site

- Now, you need to be on the same page and Click on Add Files button and then browse your audio file which you want to upload. Or click on attachment. Just

follow the instructions

Audio Song

ADD FILES

- Then it will start uploading your audio file which will take some minutes of yours to get completed. You may repeat this process to upload other audio files too but remember that limit must not exceed from 100 MB and one file of 25 MB.
- After that, you need to make it accessible for your readers and for that you need to Click on **Home** button from side bar and then select gear icon from top. Then you'll see different options out of which you need to select **Sharing and Permission**.

- Now, check if the permission is granted to Public then it is ok, if not then Click on Change button under **Who has access**.

Link to share

https://sites.google.com/site/audiofile66058/

Share link via: M $\mathbb{S}^+$ f y

Who has access

Public on the web - Anyone on the Internet
can find and view   Change...

Is owner

- Then select **On-Public on the Web** and Click on Save button.
- Now, you need to get the complete URL of audio file which you have uploaded
  and for that select the audio file right click on download button, then select **Copy
  Link Location** or **Copy link Address** (depends on your browser).

Audio Song

Open Link in New Tab
Open Link in New Window
Open Link in New Private Window

Bookmark This Link
Save Link As...

Copy Link Location
Search delta-homes for "d"

Inspect Element (Q)

01 - MANWA LAAGE.MP3   MANSOOR AHMED MEMON, ...   V.1

ADD FILES

Step3: Adding Audio Files in Blogger
To add the audio to blogger

- Go to **Blogger >> create a new post** there for your Audio file.

- Now Click On Link

- Paste The Prepared Link in URL Box, Write "Download" in "Texts to Display" Box and the link in the web address.

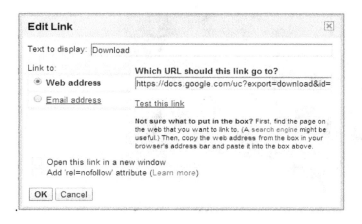

- **Click "OK"**

How To Create A Blog Page

Blog page is the list of stand alone pages that contain the relevant informations on your site. eg About us, Contact Us, privacy Policy etc.

To create A Blog Page Follow these steps:

- On The dashboard Click pages

- Click New pages;

The dialogue will open

- Enter Your page Title in the small box above, then, the full contents in the bix box, you can add as many images to it
- Then, Click Publish

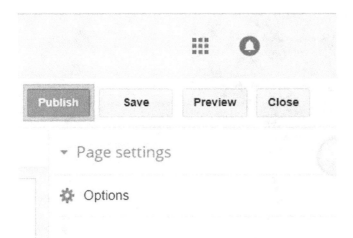

Your page will be published but will not appear on the site yet.
follow the same steps to create all your pages

Now For Your Pages To Appear On Your Site

<u>Layout</u>

You can control the widget of your site on the Layout page, Add Elements, Remove etc.
- Go to Layout On your Blog dashboard;

On this layout area, you can add any elements to your site like to place adverts, link, banner, code, etc. You can add element to any side of your site eg; the header, footer, sidebar etc and you can re-arrange the elements there.

For Your Pages To Appear On Your Site

Decide on the side you want the pages to appear; you can use the footer, if you want it to appear at the bottom or the header if you want it to appear at the top or the sidebar, if you want it to appear at the side of your site.

Click on a Add Gadget in the cross page Header if you want it to appear in a horizontal way.

Scroll down to choose pages or Any other element you want to add there.

On this section tick as many of your pages you want it to appear on the site; Note: any page that you did not ticked will not appear on the site.

If you want to link a page to another website
Click on Add external Link
Enter the Title And The Address
Save. save the element and preview your site.

How To Add Other Gadgets To a Blog

To **Add popular posts gadget;** this popular posts display the list of your popular posts
- Go to layout

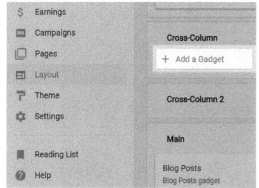

- Locate the side you want it to appear, sidebar is the best.
- Click on add gadgets;

scroll down until you see popular posts

- Click on the + sign or click on the name.

select the number of posts you want it to display and the navigation

- **save.**

To Add Search Gadget

this search gadget allow visitors to navigate into your site easily by searching for the information they need on your site.

Step to add the gadget

- On the layout > Locate the area you want it to appear

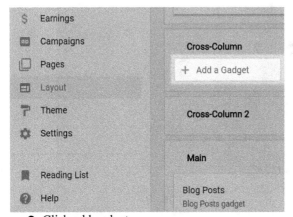

- Click add gadget

scroll until you see the search button, you can edit the name from search this blog to any name you want.

- **Save.**

To Add Label to Screen

- On The Blogger Layout

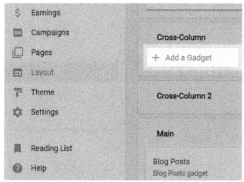

- Locate the area you want it to appear
- Click Add gadget
- Select Label from the list of the elements there

you can change the navigation you can even select the number of categories you want there.or **save** it like that.

How To Add Email Subscription Gadget

E-mail Subscription Gadget give your visitors easy navigation to your site. your visitors can subscribe with their email so that any time you make a post they will receive it in their email.

Steps To Add The Gadget

- On The Blogger Layout

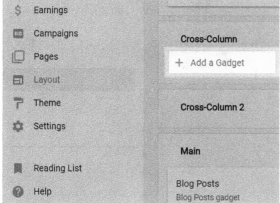

- Locate the side you want it to appear
- Click Add a gadget
- Select Follow by email or email subscription; you can edit the title; then, **Save.**

How To Add Contact Form

Contact Form Allow your visitors to give you a direct contact from your site, just by filling a short form in your site, and when they send a message you will receive it in your inbox.

To Add This gadget
- Go to the Blogger layout
- Locate the side or position you want the gadget to be
- Click Add a Gadget
- Click Add More Gadgets

Search for Contact Form if you cannot find it in the first page. you can edit the title

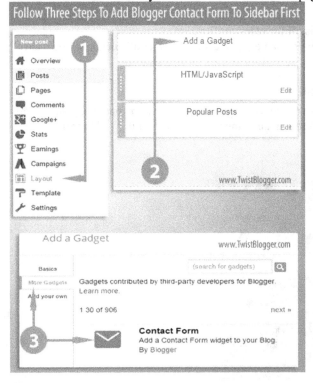

- **Then, save.**

How To Add Javascript Code

This is the place you will add Javascript Code Like: Banner, Link, Code, Adverts, animinational Code, google adsense ads etc.

- Go to Blogger Layout

- Locate the side you want the gadget to appear
- Click add New Gadget
- Select HTML Javascript

- Enter the title of the ad. eg google ad and paste the code in the bix box there,

- **Save.**

use the above steps to add more HTML gadgets, make sure you follow the instruction and you will progress.

How To Add Logo To Your Site

- Go to Blogger Layout

- Click Edit On The Header
- Upload your logo

- Select whether to replace the logo with the title and description

then, **save.** but if it's not organized you can edit it again and replace it with the *Title and Description*.

How To Rearrange Your Gadgets

To Rearrange the gadgets on your blog
- Go to Layout

- Click and hold any element you want to change the position. for example if you want the contact form to stay below the main blog posts, drag it from the position and drop it below the main blog posts.
- Then, click save arrangement.

How To Delete Element

To delete element from your site
- Go to Blogger Layout

Blogger

Configure HTML/JavaScript

Title
Author Details

Content   **b** *i* 💬 66 | Rich Text

Templatesyard is a blogger resources site is a provider of
high quality blogger template with premium looking layout and
robust design. The main mission of templatesyard is to provide
the best quality blogger templates which are professionally
designed and perfectily seo optimized to deliver best result
for your blog.

Save   Cancel   Remove

- Click Edit on the gadget you want to remove
- then, click remove.

The Element will be removed.

Blogger Post setting

There are two ways to edit the blogger post setting;

1. Go to Blogger Layout;

Click Edit on the main blog post; it will prompt you to where you can adjust your blog posts setting; the number of posts you want it to appear on the main blog page, you can also activate ads from there if you are running adsense whether ads should appear in the middle of your posts of below. adjust the setting there.

Then, Save.

2. Go to setting on your blogger dashboard

click on posts and comments; here you can also edit some posts setting; like comment setting and author profile.

How To Post on Blogger with Email

You can make post to your blog with any Email account

- Go to setting on your blog dashboard
- Click on Email

you will be asked to enter a secret word. for example my (mydomo) if your blog email is kogilatestnews@gmail.com this is how you are going to post with an email;
kogilatestnews.mydomo@blogger.com

Then, decide how it will be publish whether it should be publish immediately or save to draft.

Now to post to your blog
- Login to any of your Email account
- Click Compose New Message
- Enter the title of your article in the message subject box

Then, enter the full article in the message main box

Click attachment to add as many images you want
- Now send it to the secrete email given to you. Remember the example; (kogilatestnews.mydomo@blogger.com) your email.secret code@blogger.com.

your post will appear in your blog automatically.

How To Change Your Blog Address (URL)

- Go to setting

scroll down until you see the blog address
- click on edit, then you can change the name.

To Edit Your site Title And Description

On your blogger setting
scroll down to edit the site title and description.

How To Allow Another Person To Have Access To Your Site

- On the Blogger Dashboard Click Setting; scroll down to the last
- Click Add Author

Enter the person's Gmail Address, **Note**;it must be gmail address.
- Click Invite Authors

an invitation will be sent to the person email. when he accept the invitation, correctly he become an author to your blog.

- Now Decide whether to make him the admin or remain as the author; if you make him the admin he have equal right with you, he can even delete you if he want.

- Go to the blogger setting,

scroll down to the last; you can edit the person to become an admin to the site.

How to Edit Your Blog Theme

To Edit or change your blog design
- Go to Theme/ Templates on your Blogger Dashboard

- If you want to work on your current theme; click customize; but if you want to change the theme, select the theme of your choice. then, **apply.**
- To Work on your current theme click on customize:

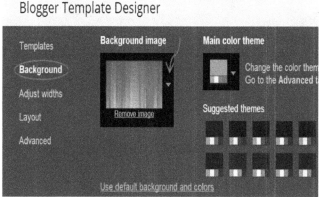

On this section you can also change your template, edit the background, edit the font size and colour. rearrange the widget and many. follow the instruction to do what you want there, make sure you click apply before you leave the section.

Chapter 3- **Advanced Blogging**

On this chapter you will learn how to create a professional blog using this advanced method.

How To Upload a Blogger Template

your template determine how your website look like. there are many free blogger templates online you can download. you can download free templates from the these websites www.btemplates.com www.gooyaabitemplates.com or search for many free and paid templates on search engine like google.com.

To Unload the template into your site
- Download the template into your computer
- The template came in zip format; right click on the template downloaded, click on extract file to extract the template. Note: if the template is not in zip format no need to extract it again. but make sure that the template you are uploading is in HTML format.
- Go To theme on your Blog Dashboard

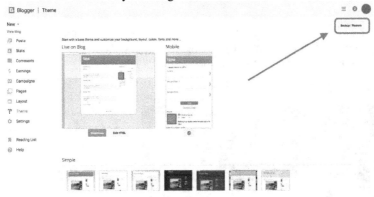

- Click Backup And Restore

Download your current theme in case of an error that might scatter your site.

- Select A Folder you want to upload from; open the folder of the template you

extracted, choose the one that have HTML format
- **Then, Upload.**

Your New Template will be successfully uploaded

Note: after uploaded new template you might experience many changes in your site, like strange pages of another website. many unnecessary gadget might be added, but don't worry, it will still look beautiful.

Go to the layout to delete the in relevant gadgets, you can also rearrange them.

Now To Delete The Pages That Follow The Uploaded Templates

HTML Templates

HTML contain the codes that control your whole site
- Go to theme on your Blogger dashboard
- Click Edit HTML

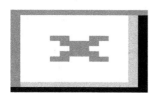

Note: backup your site before editing your HTML template, all the codes there are for a purpose, these are the codes that control your website. make sure you know what you are doing.

Now To Delete Or Replace Pages on Your Site

- Preview your site in another tab

make sure that you add a page Gadget from your layout to either the sidebar or footer, if you have not added a page gadget to appear in your site go and do it before using this.

- Now Click On one of your page. eg about us. when it opens copy all the link there.
- Now go back to the HTML Code; you can use two method to edit the code; By **Jump to Widgets or Press Control +F** to search for the gadget you want to work on.

if you Edit your HTML code by Jump To Widget; you can edit it manually, we have many sections there header, Main blog, anything that is on your site have a section. locate the one you want.Since Page is in the Header choose Header; Scroll up and down small until you start seeing the list of the pages you are seeing on your homepage there. Or press **Control+F** on your keyboard; search for any of the elements you want to change and it will appear. For Examples if you are seeing pages like:sora, ceo, download etc on your site after you uploaded the template.

You can press control+f then, search for sora, or check it manually. Replace the name "sora" with your new page name. "About us" the highlight URL inside this quotation "# " delete it and replace it with the url of the about page on your site.

Check the image below to see...

```
1    <?xml version="1.0" encoding="UTF-8" ?>
2    <!DOCTYPE html PUBLIC "-//W3C//DTD XHTML 1.0 Strict//EN" "http://www.w3.org/
3    <html expr:dir='data:blog.languageDirection' xmlns='http://www.w3.org/1999/>
       xmlns:data='http://www.google.com/2005/gml/data' xmlns:expr='http://www.goo
4    <head>
5        <link href='http://fonts.googleapis.com/css?family=Armata' rel='stylesheet
6    <!-- First Step Add jQuery - Talkofweb.com Floating Social Share Bar -->
7        <script src='http://ajax.googleapis.com/ajax/libs/jquery/1.8.1/jquery.min.
8    <!-- First Step Add jQuery - Talkofweb.com Floating Social Share Bar -->
9    <b:if cond='data:blog.pageType == &quot;index&quot;'>
```

```
115  </head>
116  <body>
117
118  <div id='navigation'>
119  <div id='wrapper'>
120      <h1 class='heading'>Talk Of Web Widget Lab</h1>
121  <ul>
122      <li><a href='#'>Home</a></li>
123      <li><a href='#'>Contact Me</a></li>
124      <li><a href='#'>About Talk Of Web</a></li>
125  </ul>
126  </div></div>
127  <div id='wrapper'>
```

- Click Save; preview your site again; that sora will be changed to your about us page.

do the same thing to change the other pages or remove, if you want to remove just delete only that specific code. Note: Highlight the page you want to edit very well before you delete.

To Change or Remove any Element Through HTML template. example: footer credit, social media link. **press control+f** or search it Normally from up to down. search for **facebook** if a facebook link is appearing on your site that you want to change or edit. you can edit all the social media that follows it or delete them.
then, save.

Use control+f to easily locate anything on your site through the html template. pls be calm and follow the instruction there. you will get what you are looking for.

Custom Domain Name

Custom Domain name is very important to every website, it make your site to look more professional.
Custom Domain Name is the name that is attached to your website name. examples are .com .org .ga. co .tv .com.ng etc.
But any domain name that have 2 dots is called a **subdomain name** eg .blogspot.com. subdomain name are usually offer free of charge while some companies give you a free domain name after purchasing a package from them like **web plan.**

How To get A Domain Name;

You can Purchase a Domain name from the following websites;
www.goddadys.com www.registeram.com www.domain.gooogle.com
www.freenom.com etc. search for more online.

How To Get A Free Domain Name

There are few companies that offers free domain names online eg, Freenom.com you
can get a free domain name from them examples .ga .tk .ml .cf etc.
- **To Register the Domain name** Visit www.freenom.com and check availability
  by entering a great domain name for your blog.

If **it is available,**
- Click on **Get it now!** button and the selected domain will be added to your cart.
- After that, Click on checkout tab.

- On the next page, change Period from 3 months to 12 months (Don't worry, it
  remains free) and Click Continue.

- Now enter your email address in the given space (as shown in picture) or you can
  use your social profile for login. If you want to sign up using email address then
  enter it and click on Verify my Email.

- Check! You will receive a confirmation link to your email address. Simply, click on that.

Congrats! You have registered your free domain.

Now It's time to set up to use it as a custom domain. For doing so, follow the steps.

To Set Freenom Custom Domain to Blogger?

- Go to your Blogger blog's Dashboard and click on the Settings tab.

Under Publishing, you will see a button like this: "+**Set up a third-party URL for your blog**", Click on that.

+ Setup a 3rd party URL for your blog - *Point your own registered URL to your blog.*

- Enter the domain name you just registered through Freenom. (along with www) and click **Save**.

It will show error, Don't worry it means that your freenom domain does not yet point to any DNS record.

- So, Go to your freenom account. On Menu bar "Domains" click on "My Domains"

- Click on Manage Domains and then Manage Freenom DNS.

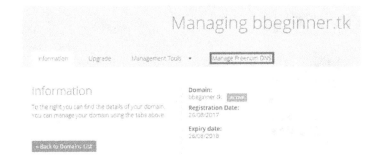

- Enter the CNAME records as shown by Blogger (in step 4)

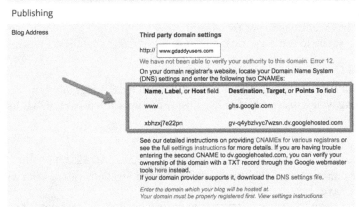

- Enter **www** in the name record, choose **cname** in the type and enter **ghs.google.com** in the target

Save that one.

Add another name Record

Enter the second dns given to you in the Record name eg **xbhzj7e22nb** choose **cname** as type, enter the second link in the target area. Eg **gv-ddswrwfwrsfsfsfs.dv.googehosted.com** see the picture of the step 4.

- Click on Save changes.
- Now, move to Blogger account (as you leave in step 4) and click on Save button again.

It will not show any error now and will get saved.

Sometimes, It may take up to few minutes to update the DNS records, so keep patience if it still shows error and tries saving it after 5-10 minutes.

Once it gets saved, Click on Edit and tick the redirect box and press **Save again.**

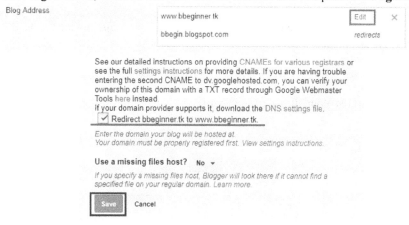

How To Add Facebook Like Box To Your Site

Facebook like box allow your visitors to directly like you facebook page from your site. This can increase the traffic of your website.

- Login To Your Facebook Account
- **Go to https://developers.facebook.com/docs/plugins/like-button**

- Enter Your facebook Page URL; do some changes if you want, include the height, the size. See the picture above.
- Click **Get Code**

Copy the two code given to you into your blogger html gadget

To place the code:

- Go to Layout On Your Blogger Dashboard

- Click Add Gadget; side the side you want to place it.

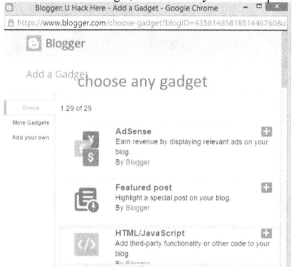

- Click HTML/ Javascript

- Type the title and paste the Code in the content box

- Save

How To link Your Site To FaceBook So That Anytime You post it will Automatically appear on Facebook.

If This then That

A new online utility has appeared that can simply move your social postings around between sites called IFTTT.com (or, in other words, If This, Then That). It is so incredibly intuitive and easy to use that I had no issues setting it up.

Visit www.ifttt.com
Register for an account, you can choose to register with your email or facebook.
Connect with facebook for quick registration
Choose connect Blogger to facebook or facebook page or any other social media you want.

- And then tie your Blogger blog to the IFTTT account:

Update
Blogger

Which blog would you like to
use with IFTTT?

Your blogs

Blogger Tips Pro ▾

Update

Once registered your first step is to 'Create a Recipe' - and in our case it is going to be from Blogger to Facebook or to facebook Page:

Create a Recipe

if this thenthat

Simply click on the blue **'this'** text to select Blogger as you source choice:

You can see that there are many options for source - I've highlighted the Blogger button. Next, just 'Choose a Trigger' type. In this case we want new Posts to be published to Facebook. However, you might want the second label option:

Go ahead and select 'Any new post' for now. Now you will see the Trigger that will kick off the event.

Just select the 'Create Trigger' button to continue. You're going to be directed now to the action that occurs when you trigger off a Blogger Post. Just select the 'that' blue link to continue:

Now you'll see the full list again of social media sites. There are some great options here - but, for our tutorial just click on the 'Facebook' icon:

If this is your first time into IFTTT then you'll need to register your Facebook account much like how you did your Blogger account. **Be sure you're logged into your desired Facebook account first.**

Now you'll have to make a selection if you want the Blogger post to be fully copied to Facebook, or, just a link back to the blog. I prefer the second option **'Create a link post'** - but you make your choice:

This is the tricky part - how you want the message formatted on your Facebook page. You can certainly experiment with this - but, you'll want to Create an Action that has the URL in the link field and the subject with your own text mixed with your blog post:

Just press 'Create Action' when done and you should have something like this:

You can see I used the Post Content field - but, you certainly don't have to fill your wall with the full Blogger post. Your connection is now ready!!

Now that your link is active you can test it by posting to Blogger, then jumping over to IFTTT.com and clicking on the Recipe you just created and selecting the **'Check'** button on the right side of the screen like so:

This normally runs every 15 minutes - but, by clicking on Check your post will appear on Facebook in seconds.

Note: The navigation of the site might change at anytime, follow the instruction to link your site to facebook.

References
Wikihow.com google.com

Thank You for reading this Book!
For More Contact me on the following:
Website: www.domotechworld.blogspot.com
Email: domotechworld@gmail.com
Phone: Numbers: +2347015118742 +2347086973998

www.ingramcontent.com/pod-product-compliance
Lightning Source LLC
Chambersburg PA
CBHW061043050326
40689CB00012B/2947